# MORNING
# LIGHT
## ON THE SPIRITUAL PATH

### WHITE EAGLE

## THE WHITE EAGLE PUBLISHING TRUST

LISS · HAMPSHIRE · ENGLAND

MCMLXXXI

*First printed November 1957*
*Reprinted June 1966*
*Reprinted June 1971*
*Reprinted December 1975*
*Reprinted March 1979*
*Reprinted January 1981*

ISBN 0 85487 018 0

*Some further books of White Eagle's teaching*
THE GENTLE BROTHER
GOLDEN HARVEST
HEAL THYSELF
THE LIVING WORD OF ST. JOHN
THE PATH OF THE SOUL
PRAYER IN THE NEW AGE
THE QUIET MIND
SPIRITUAL UNFOLDMENT I
SPIRITUAL UNFOLDMENT II
SUNRISE
WISDOM FROM WHITE EAGLE

SET IN 12 ON 14 POINT SPECTRUM

*Printed in Great Britain by*
FLETCHER AND SON LTD, NORWICH

# CONTENTS

# Introduction

THE following definition of the origin and work of the White Brotherhood is taken from a Rosicrucian source:

'It has been the privilege of the Brotherhood in all ages to transmit from century to century, from race to race, the secret heritage, the ancient wisdom, the inner truths which God and nature have revealed to man. Here, the fruit of human experience, the secret methods of unfoldment of the spiritual and physical personality of individual beings, the rituals, laws, principles and methods of self-mastery, of solving life's problems, of discovering the great truths—here have these been fostered and taught to the few.

'Always the few in every race, in every land and in every time have been the protectors of this heritage. These few have been known by various names, such as the Essenes, the Therapeutae, the Knights of the Temple, the Hermetic Brothers, the Alchemists, and the Martinists. They have formed secret lodges where they have taught humble students under various names and symbols. The work of the Great White Brotherhood has gone forward, even to this very hour.

'Every history of civilisation reveals the powerful good accomplished by such secret schools; they have ever been tolerant in their religious views, kindly and merciful in their political attitudes, free from entanglements, and always devoted to the service of mankind for the greater glory of God.'

The White Brotherhood exists on both sides of the veil, in two worlds, physical and spiritual; its representatives who pioneer on earth draw their inspiration and power from these realms invisible. It is from these realms that the contents of *Morning Light* have come. They were spoken to audiences composed of students of spiritual science, by one called by the name of White Eagle (a symbol of St. John), and represent but a fraction of the wisdom and truth received from him. White Eagle has been speaking through the mediumship of Mrs. Grace Cooke for nearly half a century. He speaks with convincing authority, yet always quietly and with humility. The printed word is powerless to convey more than a reflection of that gentle, radiant yet powerful personality whose very presence brings a blessing.

# I

# Gleam of Dawn

W E come from the life of spirit, a life beyond death, to bring you a message which will give you spiritual help, which will comfort and heal and bring peace to your hearts; a message which will answer some of the problems which confuse you at the present day. For the outer world is in a turmoil, the minds of men agitated by fear, distrust, anger, resentment, and man can find no answer to his problems, because instead of looking to the Source of absolute wisdom, he endeavours to answer all questions purely with his mental or intellectual powers, or else on the material level of life.

The answer to every human problem lies in the divine mind; and when man can rise above himself and contact the divine mind, then he will receive the guidance for which he longs. Our purpose is to help you to make this contact, and thus to find the true guidance, the true answer to the problems which perplex you.

We have spoken many times of the great need for man to understand that he has an inner, spiritual existence as well as an outer, worldly life; and it is essential that man should discover that spiritual part, and set himself to develop it. There are many schools of teaching, but only one central truth of which all else is but a part, and this truth is pure spirit. You have this pure spirit within your own being and you are here on earth to develop your spiritual self, which is in truth the Son of God, the Christ Being, lying buried beneath many coverings, physical, mental and emotional.

Do you not understand that within *you* is something more precious, more beautiful, more wonderful than man has ever conceived? Occasionally you hear stories of a manifestation of that glory through the saints or great ones; you see through them the radiance of the divine life. You think to worship, but never to draw near these great ones. You worship from afar instead of taking hold of yourself and working to perfect your own character and your own soul, so that they become fitted for the divine spirit to manifest through you to your fellow creatures. Yet this is the whole purpose of your life.

We have said that man tries to solve all the problems of the age from a purely material standpoint, and because of this he is filled with fear—fear for himself, fear of his fellows. In the new Aquarian age towards which man is advancing there will be stimulation of both the spiritual and material aspects of man. A number of souls are already in incarnation who either consciously or unconsciously have come here to be pioneers of the new age.

We would therefore have you understand that however simple, however obscure your own life may appear, you have a special mission or charge; you have come to earth for a special purpose, not only to develop your own divine consciousness, but also as a pioneer to serve the coming age.

You cannot help but develop your own character, your own innate divinity, if you do not trouble too much about your own growth or development, and instead truly serve your fellows. For when once a soul learns to recognise and obey spiritual laws, it will find itself following a spiritual pathway which seems to be already opened and prepared for it. This happens with all pioneers of the spirit, although many of these are passing through a hard time, for they have necessarily to work in comparative solitude to prepare for an influx of many Brothers of the Great White Lodge, who are presently coming to the earth. Angels too will draw near and men will walk and talk with angels. But remember, it takes an angel to recognise an angel, a god to recognise a god; so that until man has developed the necessary qualities within himself, he remains unconscious of the presence of angels or of gods.

## Truth lies within Yourself

If you would find an answer to every personal or world problem, practise the art of becoming very still within—as still and silent as the surface of a lake without a breath of wind to disturb it. This lake represents your soul, and when it is still and you have developed the will of God within yourself, then you will see without distortion the reflection of truth on the waters of the lake which is your soul or 'psyche.' 'Be still, and know that I am God!' When man is alone with God, God speaks to him. Man then sees truth reflected in his own psyche. But if man does not use the *divine* will, does not pray for the will of God to be done; if man is wilful, seeking an answer in accord with his own desires, then the answer will be distorted, for there is no peace in him, the lake of his soul is not still.

The soul of man is a wonderful instrument, and can be likened to a receiving set with which he can tune himself in to many stations; either to spheres in the grey lower astral worlds of disquiet and desire, or to spheres where all life is a manifestation of the beauty of God; and even, if he so desires, to other planets of the solar system.

Man has indeed been given wings, but has yet to learn how to unfold these wings and rise into worlds of infinite beauty.

In your prayers and aspirations you may touch a vibration of purity which you feel in your heart as simple goodness. Such a pure feeling as this does not depend upon possession of a powerful and well-stored mind but upon a pure and constant joy uprising in the heart. Every son or daughter of the living God should live joyfully. If you analyse our words you will find they are profoundly true. Take as an example your own life. If you were touching the secret of joy, and recognised and faithfully cherished in your life this pure joy in God, how different your feelings and outlook would be!

Think of the immense blessing conferred upon mankind by the soul who can live in joy and pure goodness without any thought of the result to self. The ideal, of course, is to do right because you love the right, because the joy within you, the life of the spirit within you, cannot do other than express itself as goodness.

Have you ever thought that only the goodness of individual men and women safeguards the future of the race? If there were no goodness in the world, there would be no future for man. The man or woman who lives in singleness of purpose to do good, to be good, to live happily, makes an enormous gift to unborn generations yet to come. Nevertheless, we recognise that it is not easy to do good, or even to be good yourself just for the sake of goodness alone. Please believe that we do not preach at you; we are only trying to work out a certain theme which we can presently make clearer. Again and again we say that if you can establish a foundation of joy and serenity within yourself, and express goodness in every action and in life itself, your contribution to the happiness of mankind will be beyond your power to estimate.

This can be illustrated by the life of Jesus. If you could only learn about that life in more detail, grasping its simplicity and humility; if you could realise his continual outpouring of the magical white light of heaven to help and heal, you would understand that only joy and goodness can truly release this power of the white magic. Any similar life is by its very nature continually pouring forth a divine essence.

This fact has been demonstrated by other great teachers. The Yogis of the East have also discovered the source of all true happiness and the secret of a richer life. The continual service they pour forth to mankind does not seem like labour to them. Rather is it a spontaneous and constant outpouring of divine essence.

## Man's Great Descent

Man has a wonderful journey before him. He has already travelled far. He has come forth as an unconscious but still potentially divine spark from the centre, the Godhead. He has descended through spheres of life invisible to present-day man, down and down, his soul ever taking on denser and heavier clothing, until at last he finds himself robed in the weightiest garment he will ever know—not only that body of dense flesh but also his material environment and existence, which will bow him down to the ground.

The substance of the earth itself has also been crystallising, solidifying as it descended in the scale of vibrations, so that now both the human soul and spirit and the earth itself have touched the bottom of a descending arc.

Some ardent souls on earth are already climbing again towards the heights, but many souls are still undergoing this process of gradual descent or materialisation. This knowledge may give us forbearance, and make us more patient with some of our fellows.

During his journey down through the various planes of conscious existence man has lived in states of beauty and harmony undreamed of today.

That is why legends of Atlantis and even more remote eras have come down to us. Men then inhabited bodies of a lighter, finer texture, and their souls were serene and joyous in an Eden-like world. They were like children still in contact with their heavenly Father, still remembering those Elysian Fields of happiness which they had left on their long journey into the depths of matter.

In the beginning man was born, or *breathed forth* from the Holy of Holies, or from the 'womb' of Love, Wisdom and Power. He was then entirely pure and innocent of soul. Now he is destined to learn to conquer weakness, to control matter, to overcome temptation. That is why he is here.

In this connection the story or legend of Atlas who carried the world on his shoulders is still significant; for it pictures the soul of man taking upon itself all the weight of worldliness. This burden is laid upon every soul, a burden which gradually increases until at the lowest arc of its evolution the soul is completely weighed down. At this stage it seems to be quite unaware of spheres of beauty and truth from which it came forth and to which it will eventually return.

World conditions today are again challenging the innate goodness enshrined in every human being, the goodness which is stimulating man to turn his face upwards to receive the heavenly light. He has to realise that all the secrets of the universe are hidden within his own being, waiting for him to release them.

# The Miracle of Light

You have asked us *why* the Divine Creator has decreed that the souls of men must leave a land of heavenly bliss to journey down into the world; and why that individualised soul of Everyman must presently by its own effort struggle back again to the heavenly places? You believe that if you knew the reason for your suffering and limitation, it would give you a new incentive and purpose.

Naturally there *is* a purpose when souls breathed forth by the Creator are directed down through the spheres to this dark earth—a very grand purpose. When individual man at last glimpses the Plan for the spiritual nurture and evolution of God's child—*himself*—he will live in peace and patience; for then his soul will rise to touch again the fringe of heaven. We can never over-emphasise the reality and constancy of the divine love and care of God for each human soul —the wonderful, all-enfolding Love which is far beyond all earthly understanding. It is a paradox that because of this very Love the little spark of the human soul is sent forth on its long journey earthwards.

For if the soul did not descend into the darkness of matter it might never become conscious of itself or of its latent powers, or ultimately conscious of its God. This in a few simple words explains the real purpose of the soul's journey, for under pressure from the darkness of earth in time it gradually opens, as a seed sown in the soil does under rain, warmth and sunlight. In other words, the pressure of so-called hardness, stress and evil working upon that seed (or soul) forces growth from the unconscious into the conscious state. Through many ages it grows and becomes ultimately master of matter, master of itself, and fully conscious, in matter, of the light and love of God.

So far as this earth plane is concerned, the soul must master its weaknesses both of the flesh and the emotions; it must do so because it is essential to its purpose. When it has learned self-mastery, then at last it is free, it has become fully God-conscious, and so become at-one with the Father, while yet on earth.

So you will see that there is indeed a purpose, a grand plan in the hands of the Great Architect of the Universe, a plan which is detailed and beautiful in order and design. You must learn to have patience and confidence in God.

## Life is governed by Law

Should you suffer any injustice, real or apparent, always try to remember that all human life is governed by divine love and divine law, and there is no innocent or wanton suffering. You appear to suffer unjustly, but only because you have yet to develop clear vision or clairvoyance which can reveal your past and future. Until you have done so you cannot recognise the out-working of spiritual law which is taking place, or see the play of unseen forces upon your being; nor can you understand the setting in which you —a jewel from the Father's crown—have been placed.

No man can escape either the joy or pain which he has earned. Man is like a magnet; and like a magnet attracts to himself *that which is himself*. This is inescapable law. In other words, he attracts to himself conditions similar to those which he constantly creates within himself, and which he is ever externalising from himself.

Because life is governed by a law which is always just, perfect and true, there cannot be any injustice. This you will question; but when you see things in clearer perspective you will perceive that every event in your life comes to influence your soul or to unfold your character, and that all is working together *in you* to bring forth the perfect son of God. Out of the ashes of the old life arises the new life. This is what the symbol of the phoenix indicates. This mythical bird was in earlier symbology called the white eagle.

The perfect man, the master soul, is a very wonderful and glorious being. You are that being, *in embryo*; perhaps, whenever you can remember this, your human life will seem truly worth while?

## On Miracles

You have often read about the miracles performed by Jesus and by other initiates; and you may probably agree that certain happenings in your own lives can only be termed miraculous. It is true—miracles are still happening. And why not? 'As it was in the beginning, is now, and ever shall be.' Such so-called miracles are manifestations of the power of the Light. When you better understand how the divine Light can work through and then control darkness, you will better understand how and why miracles occur.

An initiate* in time reaches a stage when he is beyond the limiting power of matter. He then becomes free to manifest through the ethers and the elements of earth, air, fire, and water. To illustrate this: the Old Testament tells how three prophets once walked through fire. Today

* An initiate is one who has become fully aware of the inner light.

also we have fire walkers, men of the East who can tread on red or white-hot ashes without injury to themselves. The materialistic ascribe this feat to some trick; the better informed say it is due to self-hypnotism! Nothing, however, destroys the fact that these men have walked through fire unharmed. The reason we give, before coming to a deeper explanation, is that the operator, having attained a degree of mastery over the atoms of his body, can transmute or raise them until they become impervious to heat.

Much the same explanation applies to walking on water, which Jesus demonstrated. Not only did he do this, but he was able so to quicken the vibrations of Peter that he also walked on the water. But you will remember that immediately the disciple's faith wavered he began to sink, and called to his Master to save him—which immediately he did.

Our point is that the Master had reached a degree of spiritual realisation where he saw his body as composed of light, and not as a solid mass as do most people; and because he was resolutely holding this thought the body became so light that it could walk on water.

The transport of an initiate from one place to another by seemingly miraculous powers is not infrequent in the East. Such a phenomenon has also taken place in London, before a number of eye-witnesses, as have other and similar cases. You may find this difficult to understand with your outer mind, but once you open your consciousness to higher realms of life, you will understand the law which enables the initiate to move his body where he will in this manner.

Man's body has also power to pass through matter. We do not, of course, seek to lessen the wonder of the miracles of Jesus when speaking of those performed by other initiates. He himself said, 'What I do, ye shall do also.' He came to teach the world that same truth which we ourselves are inadequately trying to express. All that the glory of the spiritual sunlight, shining through Jesus, was able to accomplish, will be done by all God's children when once they can fulfil the demands of the law.

Let us try to state this law in very simple words. All life consists of two aspects, which can be variously called positive and negative, constructive and destructive, light and darkness, good and evil. The two are in a way antagonistic. Everyone reacts to their influence, and feels their attraction and impulse. To illustrate this, your heart, which is your true self, longs for and believes in truth, believes in a heaven world, in a Jesus Christ, and in God's goodness; it accepts these as a little child does, feeling and knowing that they are true. Another part of you is of the earth, and pulls you down again, so that what you may believe in tonight, tomorrow you cannot spare time for.

The whole purpose of your life down here is that the spirit, *your* spirit, shall shine within earth's darkness. Your spirit is identical with the light which shone in the beginning. In the beginning of your existence you were light; and the light shone in the darkness—which is your dense body on the earth—and the earth comprehended it not. You are familiar with these words but you apply them to ages past, instead of to your own life. You do not understand that in essence you are light, a child of light. But your physical body, or what some call the mortal mind, cannot comprehend this light. You, the real you, are here for a purpose, to shine through both body and mind and transmute them. When the spirit gains control over matter, over the body, miracles happen. As the spirit becomes strong in its manipulation of physical atoms, it is able to use any of the elements at will.

This is not done by human thinking but by the quickening of a pure spiritual consciousness in man, which is all love. This means the arising, or the coming to life of the Christ spirit in man, which says, 'I am the light of the world!'

And again, 'In the beginning was the Word, and the Word was with God, and the Word was God.' 'And God said, Let there be light: and there was light.' Light is spiritually another word for life —for human life, all life. Pure light was the beginning of all creation. It is also the sustaining power of creation, the foundation of all things. Your own body, seen with the eye of the spirit, is a form composed of clear light.

Many will presently be helped to realise this by science, which has now concluded that not only is there no solidity in matter—a truth which was known long, long ago by the wise men—but has almost determined that physical matter does not really exist, that it is what the Easterners call 'maya' or illusion. We are told, however, that when the physical atom, with its electrons and protons, is examined by the eye of the spirit, it is seen that around the protons are particles of light. Thus within the physical atom the light shines, and without that light there would be no atom, and no world in which man could exist.

Here then is a simple basic explanation of how and why miracles take place. They come about because of man's developing this inner light, the light which is not only something which beautifies and illumines his heart, but a reality which permeates the very flesh which clothes his soul. It dwells within the very substance of physical matter, which the initiate controls by means of this realisation. This light will shine through, control and glorify matter. Even thus do you glorify your Father Who is in heaven.

All this may be beyond you at present, but it is your eventual goal. It means that you must not seek to escape from life with its hardships, except by making a stronger contact with God. Let God's light so suffuse your being that you are raised from darkness to light, from earth to heaven.

We say again that if you will try to purify your own bodily atoms by right thinking, right living, right feelings and actions, and by judging no man but yourself, you will raise your whole consciousness and find happiness at present beyond your dreams. Peace will rule in your heart, and a gentle and gracious power in you will make crooked places straight.

Yes, the stories of miracles contain a deep esoteric truth. They illustrate the meaning of the Master's teachings. Study the scriptures; then study the human life around you with a loving eye. Study the immensity of the heavens. Love God. Seek the inner planes of your spiritual self frequently. Follow the inner light and the path of the spirit, and you will behold the mysteries of heavenly places. Then you will clearly understand how miracles are wrought.

# III

# The Quickening Sun

We shall speak often about the qualities and nature of the light. By 'Light' we mean the Christ within men's hearts, which manifests in the God-like qualities of gentleness and patience in a soul—of hope, trust, forgiveness, intuitive sympathy with others, restraint and forbearance, and the quality of pure love from which all these arise. This is why we say, 'Love is light, and light is love.'

## Worship of the Light

Long ago we used to do all our planting of crops in accord with the light. That is to say, we invoked the blessing of the Great White Spirit on the seeds before they were planted. We directed the light into the earth itself. When men learn to do this again they will reap much finer crops with which to nourish both the body and the soul.

In ancient days men were well aware of these truths, well aware that light and love could be a power in the land. They would meet either in small bands or gather in vast ceremonies in order to worship the light. They were first taught how to do this by God-men who in the beginning came to instruct their younger brethren in such arts. Men learnt that the light that came to illumine their ways was a creation of the goodness of God; and that this light would ultimately reveal to men their homeward path to God.

Before the ceremonies the ancient people would perambulate their 'lodge,' would march with rhythmic steps and sacred song around their temple, which would be on a level place, often on a hilltop. Throughout the night they would pace around their vast temple, under an open sky lit by a myriad stars and planets in this solar system both seen and unseen—for there are planets circling the sun which are unknown to man. All present understood that their worship was directed by Angels of the Light gathered for that purpose, and indeed visible to many. , At the first light of dawn a great stillness came upon the multitude. Then at the first sight of the sun all the people turned to the light, worshipping, praising, thanking the Great White Spirit for the coming of a new day of special grace and blessing.

How many today would make time or opportunity to assemble to see the sun rise? How many could see the angelic hosts manifest in the sunrise, and all the shining ones gathered to bless the peoples of the earth? Few indeed, we think. But long ago the peoples realised that at such times they were touching the secret of the creation of life, and were receiving into their being a radiation of the Solar Logos by which they were strengthened and purified. They *breathed in* the Light which was actual life-force, and which purified, perfected, irradiated human-kind.

The ancient people inhabited bodies of a finer vibration than that of the physical form of today, in the sense that they were more attuned to the forces of nature, to the great Mother-God; more open to the spiritual forces, more open to the Light.

What is meant when it is said that a man bears a light within himself? How does that man behave? Surely, as a son of God. According to his understanding he is true to God. He who bears the light within must be true, he is a true man. He must be true, because he sees clearly. His vision is not distorted, not veiled. He sees and goes straight to truth, and gains ever fresh understanding of truth.

By this we see that the word 'light' must itself be another term for truth. Throughout the ages, it is said, God has never left man without a witness. Throughout the ages God has sent His messengers to speak truth to man. Therefore we shall find in all races, past and present, something of this teaching concerning the light. It was known during the Hyperborean Age, known by those who dwelt in the Andes, in Polynesia, in ancient Egypt and the Far East, and indeed right up to the early Christian era.

'Let the light shine!' was the command of the Egyptian high priest. 'Let the fire be lighted!' was the invocation of the high priest in the Andes; and in Atlantis we find the same invocation, 'Let the light shine!' as the priest of the great Sun Temple opened the worship. In the temples of Greece the same command was voiced. Here the temple maidens or vestal virgins were given the task of guarding a flame upon the altar, emblematic of the sun. If the light ever went out their penalty was death.

Later we come to the advent of the Solar Logos, or the Christ who spoke through the lips of Jesus saying, '*I am the light of the world.*'

## The Christ Radiance

The opening words in the Gospel of John declare, 'The light shineth in darkness; and the darkness comprehended it not.' Few people stop to meditate upon and to contemplate the beauty contained in this saying. At the beginning of creation God said, 'Let there be light!' and out of the darkness the Light shone. The destiny of every individual man is to attain full understanding of and have his being within the light of God.

When you dispose by fire of the outworn garment of man's body of flesh after death, this disposal by fire means a changing of its atoms; or in other words, a releasing of the light which was imprisoned within the atoms by the darkness. Indeed, what man fears as death is in truth a form of initiation of greater or lesser degree; at death a great light breaks upon the soul. My children, we beg you never to regard the passing of any soul from its imprisoning body into a richer life as something to be dreaded. According to the law of God, when the right time has come, the soul* goes forth, not to lose its identity but to gain a greater consciousness of God, and of the eternal light.

Thus, when a man begins to understand the nature of light, when he can receive the radiation of the light, his Christ-consciousness is stimulated. This man need not be over-intellectual or clever in order to respond. Only a simple loving person is required—that is all.

For in the degree that any person learns to practise lovingkindness towards other human beings, or loves life itself as he finds it expressed

* The word 'soul', be it understood, means the man himself—the familiar 'ourself' of feelings, likes, dislikes, interests, affections, memories, sentiments—in a word the 'we ourselves' who live inside the outer man, and look out through his eyes, speak with his tongue and lips and think with his brain.    It is this 'ourself' which survives death and migrates to a brighter realm.

in the beauty of every day, so does his light shine, because Christ radiates from him. Love, thus expressed, is drawing to the soul the sunlight of Christ, so that the truly loving soul becomes radiant.

For a moment try to contemplate the face, the form, the appearance, the whole nature of Jesus the Christ. We do not deny that there have been other world teachers who have received the light of Christ in great measure; but we hold before your vision now the great saviour of Christendom, Jesus the Christ. See in him the divinity of God, the purity and beauty of the Christ spirit; see how Jesus expressed the full glory of the Christ love; for the Christ love is Light.

Then for a moment try to imagine what heaven itself is like. Try to create heaven according to your own idea. Try to imagine a state of being constantly irradiated by golden light. See in that heavenly state beings, perhaps angelic, perhaps human. One and all will look to you as if lighted from within, for all are radiating light. Why is it that spirit people who come back from their celestial state appear as beings of light? Why is this heaven so suffused with light? Because, in its reality, life is light.

Then read in your Bible of the visitation of angels as seen by prophets and saints of old.

Was not Paul smitten by a great light and became utterly changed? Angels clothed in brightness appeared to minister to Peter. Jesus once withdrew with three disciples to a hilltop, where he and even his raiment became transfigured by the glory of the light.

These are stories told by honest and true men. They happened only yesterday, so recent is two thousand years ago in comparison with the history of man. Do you believe these things? They are still happening, and will always do so, because behind all physical form is a spiritual life-force which expresses itself as light.

Again and again we say, *Light is life,* and *life is light.* For man to retain light within he must *love.* Look at anyone you know who is loving and kind. See how a light shines through. Try yourself to see whether you can observe love expressed in other faces, even the unlikely kind of faces. Alas, when someone does not love he becomes charged with self-pity. This lets down the shutters of his soul. Then he looks dark, for his light is subdued or even covered up.

So—let the light shine! Send out the light! Go about life with a loving attitude, and your light will indeed be bright.

### *The Secret of Perfect Health*

Do you know that the life-force derived

from light and coursing through your veins is the secret of perfect health? Yes, lack of light means lack of certain elements in the bloodstream, which will eventually cause disease, sickness, and breakdown. Jesus knew this secret. He knew well how to receive the radiation from the Son of God. He did not need to touch the body of a sick person to send light into that body, for he had overcome limitations of time and space. When the centurion came to Jesus begging that his servant might be healed, Jesus had already extended his aura and healed the sick man by infusing him with vibrations of light. In other words, he took light into the darkness and dispelled it.

Light infuses even the substance of the earth. You think of your earth as dark, as dead, but in the substance of the earth, her physical matter, there is light.

The very life of God Himself expresses itself as Light; and this Light sustains the mortal life in a human body and eventually gives eternal life to man's soul. The real object of man's life, therefore, is to discover and to make use of Light, and thus become a 'sun' or son of God. Probably you are by now thinking that you have a long way to go. So have we all. But we who speak have *seen*; we know that life is essentially light, and the perfect life is the glory of God.

C

Be patient. Look forward, and never back. Turn your faces to the light and 'keep on keeping on' patiently and trustingly. In the degree that you give forth light, which is love, you will assuredly receive. Be encouraged, and not disheartened. If you are sad or suffering, we pray that you may have a demonstration of the power of God's light and love to work miracles, both in your body and your material circumstances. The law is this: God has so created His sons and daughters that *they themselves must release* the light before it can act *in* them, and in their outer lives.

Look ever to the Light, which shall overcome all shadow and set you free. Such a freedom means peace of mind and heart, happiness, and abundance of all that is needed. The time is approaching when man will be able to command the action of light over matter, and do this unselfishly for the good of all.

# IV

# The Light that is Life

THINK often over these things. Your Bible affirms that God created man in His own image. This is indeed true. Even with man's present limited understanding he can recognise God as omnipotent, omniscient and omnipresent; and one and all of you have had demonstrations of love and wise guidance which have convinced you of an intelligent and loving Power behind your life.

Sometimes, of course, this Power has directed you into situations which you dislike, and you suffer because you decide that things have gone wrong; that nothing you wished to happen has occurred. But when you become more enlightened you will no longer see things in this way. You will know that God's laws are just, perfect and true, and that whatever happens in your outer life, however undesirable it may seem to the outer mind, has always a compensating blessing behind it.

When you have been relieved of a former condition to which you were clinging, this is like a parent releasing from a baby's fingers a plaything in which the parent sees harm or danger; the baby screams, but the wise mother gently says—'No, my child, here is something better'—and offers her baby something more suitable.

Apply this illustration to your own life and its happenings and you will learn in time the value of acceptance. Try to accept what happens, knowing that God is wise in all His giving, and perhaps even wiser in His withholding or taking away. The whole point is that when the human soul evolves and expands in consciousness of God it cannot really lose anything. Only its own limited consciousness prevents the soul from recognising that *all is here, all is present.*

People who spend much time in prayer, or meditation on God are sometimes misunderstood by their fellows, who say that action is better than prayer. True, action is right at the right time, but action should result from meditation and prayer, and never from emotional stress.

### The Elder Brethren

Now we would like to tell you about the Elder Brethren who live on the heights. By 'heights' we mean an elevation of consciousness as well as remote mountainous places of the earth. These Brethren have reached a level of spiritual knowledge whereon they are in close communion with the Eternal Spirit; and from this level they work unceasingly for the spiritual illumination and unfoldment of humanity. Being so attuned to God, their own soul-consciousness expands so that they become attuned to all human life; and in this exalted state they become messengers between the Creator and His creatures.

They still retain their physical form as men and women, and having passed through all grades and degrees of human life they understand the most elementary need of any human being. They are all love and understanding. They are never severe, nor do they coerce; they leave their younger brethren in absolute freedom of choice. They worship God constantly, and through that worship radiate light and love to humanity. The majority of people do not recognise this influence radiated by these great ones; nevertheless it is constantly at work. Thus the Elder Brethren work ceaselessly for you and all men.

They are never hasty, never judge anyone. The young in soul are quick to judge, but the Brethren are patient, for they are well aware how slow is the process of soul-expansion in any of God's creatures. They never expect too much of anyone. These Elder Brethren are very close to humanity. As soon as man learns to use divine law, to act by divine law, then the channel opens wide to the inflowing power of the Christ light.

## *The World Teacher*

It is frequently asked if another World Teacher is soon to come. But you realise of course that there can be only the one supreme Son of Life? In Christianity he is called Jesus Christ. Through Jesus of Nazareth the Light once shone; through other initiates the same Light will some day shine, but on a higher spiral, a higher cycle of life.

You are probably wondering whether the World Teacher will be recognised or accepted by church or people when he appears? We wonder, for this does not always happen. Only from a distance, sometimes after the lapse of centuries is recognition given. We have to remember always that it is not the *person* of that World Teacher which is significant, but the radiation of the Christ light which shines through him. In course of time the world will begin to wonder and to worship when it sees the power and influence radiated by his life, and when it realises the wisdom of his teachings.

He draws very close to man at the present time. He brings all love, all wisdom. His mighty power and light will stimulate the subtler bodies of man; indeed, that influence is already active upon earth. This is why you see so many international difficulties and upheavals, with many a clash of ideologies; one nation wants to do one thing, one another, so that humanity is apt to behave like children in a nursery. Men react to the stimulation of this great spiritual light in different ways—why, they do not understand. They feel a tremendous urge to push forward, to assert themselves, a desire to introduce brotherhood in its crudest form. Behind all such immature expressions of unrest and quickening is the impulse proceeding from the coming light of the World Teacher.

Do not think about him as being represented by one individual only. While heavenly light and power will shine through him, its inflow will not be confined to his personality alone but will be working like leaven in the bread, and will stimulate the spirit in man, and will also quicken the vibrations of the earth itself.

The World Teacher when he comes to earth will not descend alone. He will bring with him many disciples. Many are indeed already here, working to prepare against his coming. Some of you may be of that number. Disciples are used to quicken the vibrations, to lighten the darkness in readiness for the greater manifestation. Everyman has to be raised before he can understand spiritual truth or reality. The disciples already labour to prepare the way. When at last Everyman is ready he will in truth raise his eyes to behold the dawning light.

### The Saving Grace of Christ

Human memory is very fallible and often needs reminding of truths vital to its being. You often forget your destiny, the path on which your feet are set.

You also forget that you are far more than merely a physical body and mind, and that you will not, cannot die. You will not even know when your own moment of death takes place, for you will find yourself exactly the same man when you have stepped out of your body as before. The kingdom of heaven does not mean some far-distant country to which you will go when you have shed your body. It is here with you, *now*; and you are here on earth encased in matter to earn by your labour the equipment you will need to make your own road into that glorious heavenly state, which can only be achieved by your own effort and spiritual unfoldment.

You have been told that if you truly believe in the Lord Jesus Christ he will as truly save you. Yes indeed; but not without *your own effort and co-operation, your own work upon yourself and your environment.* For is it not said that whatsoever a man soweth he shall surely reap?

Your thoughts, words and deeds are the seeds you are daily sowing all your life through. The result of this sowing is certain and inescapable. We do not preach, or try to frighten anyone; we are just giving you truth, which you can prove for yourselves very easily. If things are difficult for you tomorrow morning and you allow yourself to get upset about them, life will seem very unpleasant. If on the other hand you remember that the things of earth are not all-important, you will remain happy. If you are hasty you will get into difficulties; but if you are patient and calmly look to God for the directions you need, then all will be well.

Your thoughts and actions are like seeds, the harvest of which is certain to be reaped at some time, in the soul as well as in the bodily life; and will also shape your whole future. This is an expression of the perfect law and is inescapable.

Together with this law (sometimes called *Karma*) is a complementary law which the East calls *Dharma*. Now 'Dharma' means that an opportunity is always given by which you can make the best of all circumstances and conditions, by realising that they come to offer you an opportunity to express your highest and best.

Therefore, together with the law of cause and effect—strict, just, perfect and true—there is also the law of *Dharma,* which demonstrates God's mercy. Assuredly, God is ever merciful to His child; but He never promises that His child shall not have to work, or suffer, or will evade expiating its sins. Instead He is saying, 'My child, my love is with you and will help you.' God's love is God's mercy. God can thus heal all wounds by helping His children to pass through their self-created karma. This mercy of God is closely related to the mercy of man. In the degree that a man shows mercy to his fellows, so does God release mercy to him.

We have touched on the power of Christ to save souls. The Christ light in man is indeed his only saviour. God has endowed every one of His children with the Christ spirit, which is the saving grace of life. In this manner Christ will save all who dwell in ignorance and sin. The divine law is love, and to break that law is sin. By reason of the discomfort and pain caused by such a violation, the soul eventually gains wisdom. Ignorance of divine law is however no excuse for sin.

On the soul's path of unfoldment, service to others is of the first importance. This can be given on the inner planes as well as the outer. The first service of any soul is of necessity to God, and is expressed in worship and adoration; the second law is to love our neighbour as ourself.

### Service through Worship

This brings back the thought of the Elder Brethren, who spend their lives in worshipping, in adoring, in meditation upon God. By this act they are helping the whole of humanity, and refining the substance of the earth herself. Any quickening of the spiritual life of man does this. The Elder Brethren radiate an influence which is surely although slowly permeating both humanity and mother earth. In the same way all who truly worship and praise God are serving mankind.

The greatest of God's gifts is human life itself; and the fact that you can daily grow in awareness of a purer life, more harmonious and beautiful than anything yet known upon earth.

This also entails your having faith in the unseen influences and in these unseen brethren who are ever close to you in spirit when you prepare yourself to receive them. My children, if you would but sit quietly with minds stilled, meditating upon heavenly things, you would be inviting the unseen guest, the elder brother or sister; you would feel his or her influence.

What we tell you is true. The Brethren of

the White Light work to help you. They are ever with you. They turn your thoughts upward. Seek first the Kingdom. Seek first the contact with the Infinite Spirit. Seek only to worship and glorify your Creator. Then you can be likened to a candle light, very simple and un-assuming; but countless candle lights held up to God increase even *His* light and glory. You cannot live to yourself or for yourself. You are living to God; and as you grow, so do His light and power increase. Why did God create you in the first instance? Because God gives out continual joy and life, and eventually receives back joy and life from His children. What a grand opportunity is yours! What a gracious path opens before you! O Lord, how wonderful are Thy blessings, how beautiful Thy temples! Let us enter in, to worship for ever and for ever. . . .

# V

# The Mists Disperse

Man sometimes thinks that all the good which happens in this world has originated from himself, failing to realise that collective and individual man is only an instrument for spiritual and unseen forces which permeate his earthly life. But he has one quality which sets him apart: he possesses freewill and the right to exercise it. He has power of choice; he can respond to all that is good and lovely, or he may turn his back on these things and by following the path of self, reap nothing but disillusion and confusion.

Perhaps you will query this? You may be feeling particularly worried today, careworn, anxious, fearful. If so, just pause and think; try to look back over your past years. Review the troubles and trials through which you have safely passed, remembering too your periods of happiness. Then realise how you have been safely brought through your troubles. Realise that God has never left you without help, never left you alone. Always something has come along which has improved your conditions. Even if you cannot admit that your material conditions have improved, have you not learned lessons which have brought you some ease of mind, some mastery over self? Are you not wiser? And even if you have suffered loss, has there not been some development, some unfoldment of your spiritual nature? Through your difficulties, trials and sorrows, light has entered into you; your consciousness of a divine love and a guiding hand has grown as the result of past events.

It is therefore a mistake ever to fear the future when it can bring an ever-increasing consciousness of God, an ever-unfolding understanding of God and God's life. It is equally mistaken to fear death. There is no death! We are always saying this. Some, and perhaps most of you, think that you believe it. You say, 'Oh yes, we know that there is no death!' But *you do not know it sufficiently.* You lack the deep realisation, and the spontaneous reaction which you should have towards eternal life.

### Neither Death nor Separation

Establish in your mind that human life is essentially infinite and eternal; that there has never been a time when you were not, and there never will be. At this you will ask, 'Shall we not get tired of this ceaseless round of incarnation? Even now life is a burden!' This is why God has limited your days in the flesh; you live on earth only for a few short years which you call an incarnation, and then you leave your body as an outworn dress, and go for refreshment to your true home in the spirit.

In daily life you do not mind moving from one house to another; you may love your old house, but when you have had enough of it you are ready to go. So also you come to the point where you would like a new body; you are weary and tired of the old. Then God is kind and allows you to pass on. You are removed from an outgrown state of existence and move onward to the next state.

Once over there, finding a measure of freedom such as you had never before experienced, you can rise in spirit to enter upon a period of intense happiness far removed from the former ignorance and limitation of your earth life. Then, when you have rested sufficiently and have assimilated the lessons of your earth life, your interest in incarnation is quickened, and the time comes for you to go forth again.

Let us make it quite clear: you need never be separated from your loved ones. Where there is love there can be no separation. Love attracts love as a magnet attracts steel, and you are inevitably drawn to loved ones, both in the spirit and as you go forth to fresh incarnation. The same law operates in all worlds.

Truly, eye hath not seen nor ear heard the glories prepared by God for His child. Man's limited consciousness has as yet no power to comprehend these glories. He cannot even realise the vast range of varied existence in the animal and human kingdoms, let alone the subtler etheric, astral, mental or celestial planes which encircle and interpenetrate the earth and will be the future homes of men.

## Man earns for himself Heaven or Hell

When you pass onwards your state of existence in the next world will largely depend on how you have lived here. If the appetites of the body have been grossly indulged your subtler bodies will be correspondingly coarsened, and cannot exist in spheres of beauty and perfection.

Do not misunderstand us. You may pass on to an astral plane very similar to this. A kindly life well spent will express itself in serenity and beauty in the beyond. But if your life has been one of coarse vibration and crude appetite you will find yourself in similar conditions on the astral plane, and there will be a return to earth fairly quickly to continue the process of education and purification. Man learns in physical life to discriminate between the real and the unreal, between the worthwhile and what is worthless. As he learns to discriminate between the worthless things and the finer qualities of the spirit, he develops what is called his 'astral' body which will enable him to enter worlds of very great beauty.

Yet while the ordinary souls of ordinary people—of the dear humanity whom we love so much for all their goodness—may not know very much about spiritual law, they are kind to others, and to be kind one must be unselfish. Such people after death quickly pass through the lower astral places in a dreamlike state until they reach a brighter astral realm where they meet their friends; not only those whom they have loved and thought lost during their recent earth life, but companions they have met and loved during former lives or previous incarnations. They go to what is really a plane of reunion. Those who are left behind on earth also have a right of entry to this plane, but only if they can put aside personal grief or resentment at any loss they have suffered. In other words, only if they can so raise themselves in spirit that no lowering emotions hold them down to earth, can they reach their loved ones*.

On the plane of reunion the soul continues with its many interests, such as music, art, literature or science, gardening, and making a

* For further description of the plane of reunion, see White Eagle's book, 'Sunrise'.

beautiful home—much as it enjoyed them formerly; but every interest will become keener and its enjoyment more vivid, because the person's power of expression will be greatly enhanced.

This process of passing away from the physical body, of traversing the planes of life and then at the right time returning, continues usually for a long time; but not necessarily so. It is possible to make rapid progress through the planes and afterwards gain eternal freedom. Nevertheless, until the soul has outgrown its lower nature and the lower desires, it must continue its earthly lives; but once it has outworn these experiences it becomes eternally free.

Yet there are those who of their own free-will reincarnate in order to help and serve humanity. Some are lowly men and women who live humbly and obscurely among the masses. They have their part in the plan. Others are initiates, masters spurred by a high ideal and purpose. We would emphasise the love and tenderness of those Elder Brethren who have traversed the selfsame path that the younger soul must walk. They understand, and never spare their help to any soul labouring on the upward path.

### Longing for God

When once the soul has quitted the astral

plane of reunion in order to pass onwards and upwards through planes and places of a wondrous loveliness, that are indeed beyond description, it becomes able to see, feel and know, to a limited extent, the love and glory of God. That is when that soul most realises its own inadequacy, its own unworthiness. The intensity of the radiation from God brings about this revelation. 'Nearer my God, to Thee; nearer to Thee!' is now its one heartfelt cry. Eventually its longing to approach that beauty grows so intense that it will do anything, or sacrifice all, to realise that longing. Then a teacher will come to the soul. 'My child,' he asks, 'you want to get ever closer to the heart of God, to become ever more like God? Then you must get back to earth to learn. This is the only way.'

You may not accept these words with your outer mind. Your intellect may doubt or deny what we say. Look deep into your heart, however, and there will be no doubting there. When you have learned to search the deeps of your innermost being, you will know that you want more desperately than anything else to be *at-one with your Father God*. You will know that God's light is reaching you all the time. It brought you back again into incarnation; it will take you onward into greater light if you will be true to its guidance. 'I am the light of the world,' said the

Christ speaking through the Master Jesus. 'I am the light. I am the light which lighteth every man to the kingdom of God.' One day you will accept this as an expression of entire truth.

'Underneath are the everlasting arms!' Strange it is to find how many people refuse the comfort of those everlasting arms! Yet infinite all-enfolding love is an ever-present reality. God is everywhere, is in everything. There is no place where God is not; no human heart need ever be bereft of God. He suffers with man in the depth of hell, rejoices with him in the highest heaven. Is it not said that every hair of our head is numbered; not a sparrow falls to the ground without His grief and mercy?

The sky over our world is high and clear, golden with shining light. Let us leave the shadows, and look up into serenity, peace and joy. Are we not children of the Light?

# VI

# A Clear and Golden Sky

## Right Thought

W<small>E</small> would impress upon you the importance of right thought, of thoughts of goodwill, of God thought. Because if this beneficent habit became strong in humanity, with all peoples earnest in prayer for the coming of goodwill and harmony, help beyond measure would go to the White Brethren who are planning the future of mankind. Indeed, we are able to tell you that the light has already broken down some of the shadows, and that a clearer understanding is coming.

Nevertheless there is still much to be done before men are freed from the shackles of their ignorance. We must all be of the one spirit, the spirit of love, the spirit of Christ. This is only attained by continual effort to be as God created and wills you to be, sons and daughters of the Light.

We see a future when wars between nations will cease. We see an entirely fresh way of life opening for man, a state of being which today he cannot even conceive. But remember that all social, industrial, national and international problems can only be solved by love; by love finding expression in patience, forbearance, service—in a word, by man living in fellowship and brotherhood with his neighbour.

Already man is learning that the good of others comes even before his own good; so that out of sore travail and pain the spirit of brotherhood is slowly but definitely being born.

Throughout his life man's thoughts are actively creating his world about him. His thought of today will be externalised in his environment of tomorrow. Thus, when people think angrily about other nations, and when that form of collective thinking becomes strong enough, war comes about, and this solely as a result of man's mass-thought externalised and made manifest. All human life is a process of thought. What you think about, *you* must in time yourself become. What the world is thinking today will surely come about tomorrow. Everything in your physical world has eventuated because it was first created in some man's thought-world.

## All-Enfolding Love

We come into your midst bringing a love which we find inexpressible in words. We only pray that the Great Spirit of love will use us as instruments to convey to you a realisation of the all-enfolding love and protection of God, of which you stand in so much need. We are speaking to you collectively but also individually because we are aware of your fears, your anxieties, and of your heart's hunger. Would that we could raise you from the earth-bound consciousness which so often imprisons you.

Never think that we cannot enter into your troubles, or understand the weariness of the body and the anxiety of the mind. Never think that we are unconcerned by your mental or material troubles. Every secret of your souls is known to the Masters. They work as with one mind, in complete unison; but when they descend to the level of humanity each has his own particular branch of work. Yet at the highest all Masters are *one*. This is because the master-mind is in complete attunement with the universal mind, where truth abides. Radiations of truth go forth from this centre to envelop the whole universe and every individual life.

The angels and the Christ himself are not so remote as you are apt to think. You have the power—even at this very moment!—to leave all to follow him, so that you can abide with him in his high estate. Try to remember this, more particularly when you are bowed down by material troubles and cares; for it is then that he calls, saying, 'Leave all and follow me . . . for I AM the way, the truth and the life.'

Men and women make such a mistake when they think of heaven as remote, as far beyond their attainment. Heaven is within man, and he must learn to find heaven while he is still in a physical body. Then he will surely migrate to a heavenly plane when he slips off his coat of skin at physical death.

### *You are never alone*

Never think that you are alone in your difficulties. We have in mind those of you who are 'up against it' at this moment, not knowing where to go or what to do. You are blindfolded, but only temporarily. Contain yourself in confidence and peace, longing only to be His servant, praying that you may be still, and await His commands. All is known to God and His agents.

For while no soul is left in isolation, yet every soul must pass through its initiation alone. Every soul must also pass from one state of life to another alone. It is this very aloneness, this mist which shrouds the future, which eventually forces the soul to progress.

For at first the soul is like a child thinking it is self-sufficient, believing itself able to accomplish anything and everything, capable of solving on its own the puzzle of living. Through loneliness it discovers the true Source of its strength. Indeed, on occasion that soul will specially need to be alone; for when the long-blinded eyes at last open and the soul's expansion or quickening takes place, it must be in solitude. This may happen to you: perhaps in this period of bondage you are purposely being left to yourself in order to develop your inner strength and faith in God.

What is this faith? Faith is an *inner knowing* that God can never fail in goodness and love. Every soul must develop this faith in God; not only this inner knowing that God is good, but also faith in the God *within itself*. Encased as you are in materialism, you are very easily misguided. It is as if a descending shutter had blacked out your awareness of the spiritual life about you. That is why earthly matters seem to you far more important than heavenly. Your real self is battened down in the hold of your own ship of life. That ship is your soul, which is being tossed hither and thither on the seas of emotion until in your extremity you cry out to awaken the Master of the ship, the Christ. On the instant he arises and says, 'Peace; be still!' and the turbulent emotions subside and all is peace.

## Inner Worlds

It is impossible for you to comprehend eternity with your finite mind; but you can listen when we tell you that deep, deep within, you can become aware of the existence of worlds of unbelievable perfection; and that as you learn to command yourself, your fears, your emotions, your anxieties, as you learn to enter into the sanctuary of peace, so you will see the glories of these worlds revealed.

The Revelation of John gives a description of the golden city with golden streets and gates inlaid with jewels, the new Jerusalem. What is this city other than a portrayal of the inner self, of the pure soul of the initiate? For here his form is symbolised by the temple, his chakras or soul-centres are the gates studded with wondrous jewels, his heart the throne for the Lamb of God, the Christ.

So also in the Gospel of John you can read a clear exposition of the soul's long journey through mortal life and of the heavenly places which await it.

The earthly mind cannot yet comprehend these matters, for man's understanding is limited by his persistence in living for himself alone. But there are some who strive to live for others, and fewer still who live only for God, in God and with God. Some, on occasion, can touch the hem of His garment. Then—*they know*. Truly, these things of which we speak are the real things both of your life and ours.

*Break your Bonds*

We, who speak to you from the spirit life, are full of love and compassion for you, for we see you in bondage, immersed in a materiality through which you long to break. My children, your prison is of your own choice, and is in reality the very condition your soul needs to prepare it for initiation. We know that you are yearning for that knowledge which alone can set you free; are longing to feel that you are close to God. You want this knowledge so that you may be a better servant of humanity; and yet you feel that you are making but little progress. But if you could truly examine yourself in one year's time from now, and if you could better assess the value of your human experience, you would say, 'Thank God for all the experiences which have helped me to progress thus far.'

You have to take this progress on trust. It is better that you should be blindfolded while you are serving your probation here on earth; for it is your attitude of mind to your hardships, restrictions and problems which is the great initiator, and which will eventually free you— and not through death—from the limitations of the mortal state.

As you are on earth so you are here in the world of spirit in which your guides, teachers and loved ones live; they come back to love you, to try to help you and lift you up when you are in despair.

Incidentally, when you can thus open yourself to receive the inner light it begins to 'iron out the creases' from the physical body and your aches and pains depart. People grow old because of their unruly emotions, because of anxieties they permit to overrule and thus possess them; they become sick because emotional stress in time overstrains the body. If you were always attuned to the Great White Light there would be no sickness.

### *Brotherhood*

This is the picture of your world with its human kind that we would paint for you. We would show you that every human soul, low and high, is linked to others as in a chain of brotherhood. Over all is the guardianship of an unseen White Brotherhood composed of lofty souls who have humanity in their charge. From these Brothers it is possible for man to receive communications. Step by step the message comes down; while we are speaking we are aware of other influences behind us, making use of us to convey their truths. Behind and above again are other influences and yet others, and so on, through the spheres; from earth to heaven this chain of communion exists.

Every one of you has your own guide of your spirit as well as your guardian angel, and you can be helped beyond all your dreams if you will go with a humble spirit into the inner sanctuary and pray, not in a self-pitying way, and not for self-gratification, but that you may fit yourself to be a true servant of humanity. Before you is the example of the Great Ones who have served humanity down the ages. They were formerly men and women who felt and lived as you.

This then is your way of life—to live not only to enjoy yourselves but to beautify, to benefit the earth and its people, and to help forward the spiritual evolution of all life. This is a responsibility laid upon each living soul by its Creator; because the whole community depends for its progress on each individual soul which quickens with God.

### Rise in Spirit

And now before we close, we would raise you in spirit into the presence of Jesus the Christ. Visualise him as he stands before you in all his heavenly glory, within the arc of the angelic hosts. He brings the message which has been brought by all the ancient ones throughout time: Children, love one another; love God the

Almighty Eternal Spirit and all His creation. And in His love you shall learn all the mysteries of your own being, of God and of the universe.

*    *    *

See the responsibility that lies with you and what a glorious opportunity is yours! Do not allow the darkness of earth to deny you your birthright of entering into the life of freedom and happiness, of service and worship of your Creator, the King of Glory. Peace and a great joy be with you!

## THE WHITE EAGLE PUBLISHING TRUST

LISS · HAMPSHIRE · ENGLAND